Contents

6140089301

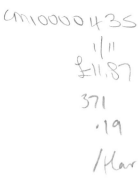

School–community–university partnerships
for a sustainable democracy:
Education for democratic citizenship
in Europe and the United States of America

Matt Hartley

Ted Huddleston

Council of Europe Publishing

Cover design and layout: Documents and Publications Production Department (SPDP), Council of Europe
Cover photo credits:
Top row – Council of Europe/Aurora Ailincai
Middle row (left to right) – Council of Europe/Emir Adzovic, University of Pennsylvania Graduate School of Education, European Training Foundation/Ard Jongsma
Bottom row – Shutterstock

Council of Europe Publishing
F-67075 Strasbourg Cedex
http://book.coe.int

ISBN 978-92-871-6795-8
© Council of Europe, November 2010
Printed at the Council of Europe

Executive summary

In recent years there has been a growing interest both in Europe and the United States of America regarding the ways in which civic skills and values can be nurtured and supported in society.

Schools and universities have an important part to play in this process. Working in partnership with each other and with local authorities and other civil society organisations, schools and universities have the potential to influence their communities for the better in many different ways. Yet this potential remains largely untapped in practice.

School–community–university partnerships for a sustainable democracy: education for democratic citizenship in Europe and the United States of America is a new publication designed to support school–community–university partnerships based on the practices and concept of education for democratic citizenship (EDC), to explain how such partnerships might be built and nurtured, and to outline the challenges they might encounter and how these may be met. It argues that, properly conceived, partnerships of this kind have much to offer, both in terms of community problem solving and in the development of more civic-minded citizens and respect for democracy in community life.

Creating EDC partnerships, ones that are truly "civic" in nature, requires particular ways of working and forms of relationship between partners, and the recognition that the process of community problem solving is often as important as its product. It requires a *modus operandi* based on participation and inclusion, a high level of reciprocity between the different organisations concerned and the desire to build stronger and more sustainable forms of democracy.

The publication is aimed at policy makers and practitioners in schools and universities, civil society organisations and community groups, and representatives of public authorities and local government bodies in Europe and the United States of America with an interest in the promotion of democratic citizenship and civic engagement.

It draws on examples of practice in both Europe and the United States of America, showing how each can learn from the other. It is the result of a collaborative effort between writers and researchers from both continents, instigated and supported by the Council of Europe through its Education for Democratic Citizenship and Human Rights programme in co-operation with the International Consortium for Higher Education, Civic Responsibility and Democracy.

Acknowledgments

This publication is a product of two years of reflection and exchange that is based upon co-operation between two long-standing Council of Europe programmes relating to education for democratic citizenship (EDC) and higher education. It also involves a new geographical perspective, in particular with partners in the United States of America.

As such, it was necessary to consult with a wide range of actors. This idea had its genesis on both sides of the Atlantic: on the European side, through the Council of Europe Chair of the Steering Committee for Education (CDED), César Bîrzea, and his counterpart in the Steering Committee for Higher Education and Research (CDESR), former Chair, Krzysztof Ostrowski; and on the side of the United States, through the driving role played by Ira Harkavy, Associate Vice President and Founding Director of the Barbara and Edward Netter Center for Community Partnerships, Office of Government and Community Affairs, University of Pennsylvania. I would also like to thank Henry Teune, a political scientist at the University of Pennsylvania, who was involved in the early stages of the project and helped pave the way for future co-operation.

After initial brainstormings in Philadelphia and Strasbourg, the cross-Atlantic reflection was launched at a meeting in San Diego, California (combined with the annual American Council on Education conference). In addition to the people cited above, I am also grateful to the following people who helped to flesh out the ideas for this publication: Aleksandra Vidanović, whose knowledge of relationships among non-governmental organisations and local authorities in Europe was particularly helpful; Susan Robinson, who brought the conversation back down to reality when it (sometimes) became too abstract; and Virgílio Meira Soares, who acted as the bridge between the higher education and EDC programmes. I would also like to thank Martina Vukasović, who helped identify some examples of EDC partnerships, and our intern Katherine Dydak.

The Ad Hoc Advisory Group on Education for Democratic Citizenship and Human Rights, and in particular its bureau, also contributed to the publication's development.

Within the Council of Europe Secretariat, I am grateful to the ongoing support of the two heads of department with overall responsibility for these programmes: Ólöf Ólafsdóttir and Sjur Bergan. I would also like to thank Alexander Bartling for his very helpful input from the perspective of local authorities, and Heather Courant, who provided the administrative support for the series of meetings on both continents with her usual efficiency and kindness.

Last but not least, I would like most of all to thank the two authors, Matt Hartley and Ted Huddleston. It was a great pleasure to work with them and I have learned a lot not only from their rich experiences, but also, and perhaps most importantly, from their overall approach during this process. It has been a truly enlightening partnership, carried out in an atmosphere of mutual respect, intellectual rigour, goodwill and transparency.

Sarah Keating-Chetwynd
Project team leader
Council of Europe

Preface

Democratic values and practices have to be learned and relearned by each generation in order to adequately address the challenges of the times.

In recent years there has been a growing interest, both in Europe and the United States, in finding ways to nurture and support the development of civic skills and values among citizens. These efforts have arisen within the context of emerging and re-emerging democracies in the aftermath of the collapse of communism in eastern Europe. They also reflect concerns within the older established democracies on both sides of the Atlantic about increasing levels of political apathy, and distrust of politicians and the political process, especially among younger people.

In both Europe and the United States it has become abundantly clear that democracy cannot be taken for granted. Strengthening democracy means far more than encouraging participation in formal processes such as voting: it means advancing a form of association or "way of life"[1] which has its roots in community and neighbourhood life and relationships. Civil-society organisations, such as national or regional ministries, local authorities, municipalities, non-governmental organisations (NGOs) and private foundations, therefore have a key role alongside government in fostering democratic values and practices.

Schools and universities have long been recognised as having an important part to play in upholding democratic institutions and practices. Schools are community institutions par excellence. They are situated at the heart of community life both physically and socially. Together with institutions of higher education they form a "strategic subsystem", which perhaps more than any other has the capacity to influence the functioning of society as a whole.

Yet while the civic potential of schools and universities has often been stated, it has not always been realised in practice. In Europe research suggests the existence of a considerable "implementation gap" at all levels and in all sectors of education, between policy intentions and practice in this field.[2] Similarly, despite the considerable interest in "service learning" in the United States, the emphasis in American schools and colleges has tended to be on the curricular benefits rather than the potential for fostering democratic values and practices.[3]

---

1. Dewey, J. (1916). *Democracy and Education: An Introduction to the Philosophy of Education.* New York: Macmillan.
2. Bîrzéa, C., Kerr, D., Mikkelsen, R., Froumin, I., Losito, B., Pol, M. and Sardoc, M. (2004). *All-European Study on EDC Policies.* Strasbourg: Council of Europe.
3. Colby, A., Ehrlich, T., Beaumont, E. and Stephens, J. (2003). *Educating Citizens: Preparing America's Undergraduates for Lives of Moral and Civic Responsibility.* San Francisco, CA: Jossey-Bass; Hartley, M. and Soo, D. (2009). "Building democracy's university: university–community partnerships and the emergent civic engagement movement." In Tight, M., Mok, K. H., Huisman J., and Morphew, C. C. (eds), *The Routledge Handbook of Higher Education.* New York, NY: Routledge Press, pp. 397-408.

Moreover, while examples of school–community and university–community partnerships can be found, especially in the United States, in neither the United States or in Europe are there significant numbers of partnerships that draw together the resources of schools, universities, community members and organisations on issues of shared concern. Such multifaceted partnerships have the potential to considerably benefit everyone concerned. Communities can help universities to ground their academic work in everyday practical reality and make learning more relevant. Sociology students can come to understand the complex issue of homelessness by working with professionals in the community that serve this population rather than by merely reading a textbook. Schools can provide physical facilities and equipment to community groups thus becoming sites for community activities. Universities can provide technical and research-based support for both schools and local communities in dealing with the issues facing them.

To fulfil its civic potential, school–community–university partnering requires a different approach from that found in school–community or university–community projects. Firstly, such partnerships must place an emphasis on the development of the civic skills and capacities of participants as well as the solving of specific problems. Secondly, they require the creation of reciprocal relationships between schools and universities and their local communities, instead of the more usual "one-way", or "top-down" model. Thirdly, they must focus as much on the process of problem solving as on the intended product or outcome of the partnership. This need not entail the creation of a completely new form of community engagement programme. It does, however, mean making existing types of programme more participatory and inclusive – for example by recognising and valuing the contributions of the different partners equally and encouraging and enabling communities to play a more active part in the definition and solution of the problems that face them – and building elements of participation and inclusion into new programmes as a matter of course.

Introduction

The purpose of this tool is to highlight the potential of school–community–university partnerships to contribute to the solution of social problems and foster democratic values and practices in local communities in Europe and the United States.

It sets out to support such partnerships, to explain how they might be built and nurtured, the challenges they can encounter and how these may be met.

The publication is aimed at policy makers and practitioners in schools and universities, civil society organisations and community groups, and representatives of public authorities and government bodies on both sides of the Atlantic with an interest in the promotion of democratic citizenship and civic engagement.

It draws on examples of practice in both Europe and the United States, showing that each has much to offer the other, and is the result of an ongoing collaborative effort between writers and researchers from both continents, instigated and supported by the Council of Europe through its Education for Democratic Citizenship and Human Rights programme in co-operation with the International Consortium for Higher Education, Civic Responsibility and Democracy.

Intercontinental collaboration is a relatively new departure in this field and poses a number of problems for joint working, not least on account of the varying traditions of discourse found in the different contexts. The terms "human rights" and "human rights education", for example, though widely used in Europe, are rarely encountered in the American context. More typical of the American approach is a reliance on the language of "civil rights", "equity" and "diversity". Similarly, the term "civic", as used in phrases such as "civic partnership" or "civic engagement", tends to be defined much more broadly in the American than in the European context. For example, in the United States a group of businesses coming together to build a new leisure centre might be described as a "civic" partnership not because it relates to the rights and responsibilities of democratic citizenship in some way, but simply because the leisure centre will be used by members of the public.

The need to bring these important differences in discourse to light as well as to prevent potential misunderstanding on the conceptual level has to some extent determined the choice of language and structure employed in this publication. Firstly, to prevent confusion we have used the expressions "education for democratic citizenship" and "EDC" as umbrella terms to include what in the European context would normally be described separately as "human rights education". In the European literature the promotion of "democracy" goes hand in hand with the promotion of "human rights". The apparent lack of reference to "human rights" in this publication should not be seen as an attempt to minimise the importance of this distinction, therefore, but as a consequence of the need to find unambiguous forms of language that help to further intercontinental understanding.

Secondly, we have coined the term "EDC partnership" to capture what is distinctive about civic partnerships based on the Council of Europe concept of "education for democratic citizenship" – that is, partnerships that exist not only to pursue specific goals but also to foster democratic (and human rights) values and practices – and to distinguish these from civic partnerships in the more general sense typically found in American usage. There can be many types of EDC partnership: school–community–university partnerships are just one.

Thirdly, we have thought it important to introduce an element of explanatory narrative into the basic structure of the publication, alongside the practical guidance it offers.

The publication begins with an exploration of why citizenship is high on the current political agenda in Europe and the United States today, and an outline of the Council of Europe's response to this agenda through its work on education for democratic citizenship – a lifelong educational process for creating democratic citizens through democratic practice. It goes on to compare this with "service learning" and other school- and college-based methods for encouraging civic engagement that are practised in the United States.

The tool then sets out a rationale for new forms of civic partnering bringing together local schools and universities with groups and organisations in their neighbourhoods, and identifies the key elements in and success criteria for such partnerships.

Finally, the tool explores the mechanics of school–community–university partnerships in practice, considering how they are built and what makes them work, and concludes with two longer case studies – one each from Europe and the United States. Not many case studies were included in the publication as such partnerships are still in the early stages and being constructed. It is hoped that this tool will act as an inspiration for potential partners through its description of good practice and step-by-step approach.

Chapter 1

The need for a more sustainable democracy

1.1. Why should we be concerned about citizenship?

Democratic values and practices have to be learned and relearned to address the pressing challenges of every generation. To become full and active members of society, citizens need to be given the opportunity to work together in the interests of the common good; respect all voices, even dissenting ones; participate in the formal political process; and cultivate the habits and values of democracy and human rights in their everyday lives and activities. As a result, citizens come to feel useful and recognised members of their communities, able to participate in and make a difference to society.

However, in recent years concerns have arisen both in Europe and the United States about the level of commitment of citizens to democratic ideals and values, and their capacity for participation in democratic practices and processes. Researchers in the UK,[4] for example, have noted the existence of what has come to be known as "the millennial generation", a generation of young people who have little interest in politics, particularly party politics, or belief that voting in elections will make a difference, and who consistently hold low expectations of government.

In Europe, democracy is often seen as coming under threat from forces as varied as globalisation, international terrorism and the effects of economic recession, as well as the effects of widespread demographic change and migration, particularly through the European Union (EU) enlargement and integration process. There is also ethnic conflict, nationalism and increasing levels of anti-Semitism, xenophobia and other forms of intolerance as well as insufficient understanding of how the European institutions work.

Similarly, in the United States, over the past couple of decades a number of factors have contributed to a sense of unease about the state of democracy, including low levels of knowledge about how the government works, increasing percentages of citizens who are sceptical about government and who believe that special interests control it, and historically low voting rates. Of particular concern has been the political disaffection of America's youth. Trend data from the Higher Education Research Institute at the University of California, Los Angeles (UCLA), which surveys a couple of hundred thousand first-year college students annually, show that the percentage of incoming students who feel it is important to keep up with political affairs dropped from 57.8% in 1966 to 25.9% in 1998, though more recent data suggest renewed interest in politics.

---

4. Pirie, M. and Worcester, R. (1998). *The Millennial Generation*. London: Adam Smith Institute.

In the light of such challenges it has become clear that although democracy has had a certain amount of resilience in the past it is by no means certain that it can survive unaided in the future. The promotion of democratic citizenship – or "civic engagement", as it is more commonly called in the United States – has thus come to be seen as a priority both in the United States and in Europe.

1.2. What does the European concept of "education for democratic citizenship" have to offer?

In Europe the term "education for democratic citizenship" refers to a set of educational practices and activities designed to encourage and help people play an active part in democratic life and exercise their rights and responsibilities as citizens in society.[5]

In many countries the use of this term represents a radical departure from traditional forms of civic education, in particular in its emphasis on active participation, learning by doing, lifelong learning, partnership working and a more collaborative and reciprocal relationship between teachers and learners.

The concept originally arose in response to the horrors of the Second World War, and was further developed in the context of fundamental changes that were taking place in a range of European countries and of the new and complex challenges faced by established as well as emerging and re-emerging democracies in Europe at the end of the 20th century. The prime mover was the Council of Europe, the oldest and largest intergovernmental organisation in Europe with 47 member countries. The concept was formalised in the Education for Democratic Citizenship (EDC) project, set up in 1997 in response to the Second Summit of the Heads of State and Government of the Council of Europe. The project had the aim of identifying the different capacities individuals require to become fully participating citizens in society, the ways in which these capacities are acquired and the methods by which they might be passed on to others.

The first phase of the EDC project (1997-2000) was conceived as an exploratory phase aimed at developing concepts, definitions and strategies. The second phase (2001-2004) was devoted to policy development, the creation of networks and communication and dissemination activities, and started to include a stronger dimension of human rights. The third phase (2006-2009) focused on policy, democratic school governance and teacher training, in particular the development of practical

---

5. "Education for democratic citizenship" means education, training, dissemination, information, practices and activities which aim, by equipping learners with knowledge, skills and understanding and moulding their attitudes and behaviour, to empower them to exercise and defend their democratic rights and responsibilities in society, to value diversity and to play an active part in democratic life, with a view to the promotion and protection of democracy and the rule of law. This definition is taken from the Council of Europe Charter on Education for Democratic Citizenship and Human Rights Education adopted in the framework of Recommendation (CM/Rec(2010)7 of the Committee of Ministers www.coe.int/edc.

tools and manuals.[6] The future programme (2010-2014) will focus on supporting policy development and implementation, promoting partnerships and networking and putting Council of Europe instruments into practice.

From the very outset, the EDC project has pioneered the practice of social partnering, and has brought together a number of different partners – member state governments, United Nations (UN) agencies, the Organization for Security and Co-operation in Europe's Office for Democratic Institutions and Human Rights (OSCE/ODIHR), the EU, different sectors of the Council of Europe, NGOs, academics and foundations. The Council of Europe worked on the premise that education for democratic citizenship is a complex and multifaceted task which cannot be left to formal institutions alone, but requires the involvement of a range of actors and agencies, formal and non-formal, state and civil society.

The idea draws on a number of innovative educational practices developed in Europe in response to the challenges to democracy experienced in different communities, countries and regions over the period, in particular human rights education, but also peace education, intercultural education and global education. These practices are a reflection of different priorities in different settings in Europe and informed by the work of governments and of national and international NGOs. They both exist alongside and integrated into more traditional forms of civic education. Although they sometimes differ in focus and implementation, the long-term goals of these "educations" have much in common, all looking to the achievement of sustainable forms of democracy based on respect for human rights and the rule of law. It is helpful, therefore, to think of each of these approaches as making a distinctive contribution to the overall aim of education for democratic citizenship, and of education for democratic citizenship as an umbrella term for a set of educational practices designed to achieve this aim.[7]

At the heart of the Council of Europe EDC project lie the three core values that historically have defined the work of the Council of Europe: democracy, human rights and the rule of law. Central, too, is an emphasis on active participation – on the part individuals can play in the democratic process, both formally and through the activities and institutions of civil society. At a practical level, therefore, the aim is to help individuals develop the knowledge, understanding, skills and attitudes needed to be able to play an effective part in society – locally, nationally and internationally. This begins with a sense of belonging, coming to feel that one is a member of society with equal rights and responsibilities and able to have an influence on and make a difference to what happens in the world. It involves the acquisition of a certain level of civic knowledge, for example about the institutions and processes of democratic government and fundamental human rights. It also involves the ability to think critically and analytically about society, that is, for people to be able to think for themselves rather than let others do the thinking for them. But democracy

---

6. Please see the Council of Europe's website: www.coe.int/edc for further information.
7. Duerr, K., Spajic-Vrkas, V. and Martins, I. F. (2000). *Strategies for Learning Democratic Citizenship.* Strasbourg: Council of Europe.

is more than a body of knowledge or set of thinking skills. It is a way of living in community with and relating to others, and demands a whole range of distinctive attributes and attitudes, from tolerance and respect for the rights of others to the ability to resolve disputes in a peaceful and friendly way, find common ground and negotiate agreements.

Thus democratic citizenship cannot simply be taught formally: it has to be learned, at least in part, through experience. Education for democratic citizenship cannot, therefore, be restricted to civic education lessons in the classroom or to the years of compulsory education: it is a lifelong process beginning, ideally, in the family, then kindergarten and nursery school and continuing through further and higher education and into adult education, vocational training and the workplace.

While education for democratic citizenship cannot be restricted to the institutions of formal education – community initiatives also have much to offer, for example – formal education is essential to the EDC project. This is not only on account of the relatively universal nature of formal education or because of its capacity for the provision of formal curricula, but also because of the opportunities it can provide for pupils, staff and others to become actively involved in their governance and their relationship with the communities that surround them, that is, to experience democracy in action.

The opportunity to experience democracy and human rights in action goes to the heart of education for democratic citizenship. Kindergartens, schools and universities need to look beyond the content of their curricula, therefore, to see how they can create such opportunities. They fall, broadly, into three categories in relation to the three overlapping kinds of citizenship learning environment, or "communities", provided in the institution: the community of the classroom, course or teaching group, the community of the school or campus as a whole and the wider community of which the school or campus is a part (as shown in Figure 1).

Figure 1: Three overlapping "citizenship learning environments"

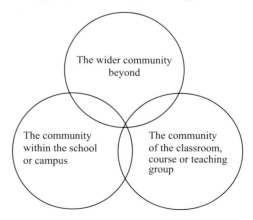

The need to create learning opportunities of this sort has important implications for educational institutions and the way they relate to other agents of education for democratic citizenship in society. Firstly, it requires a "holistic" approach in which education for democratic citizenship is seen as "both a subject and more than a subject". Secondly, a more democratic form of governance is called for, in which all "stakeholders", young and old, teachers and learners have a role to play, through the introduction of more democratic management systems and shared responsibility for school improvement and decision making. Thirdly, it requires an emphasis on active and experiential methods in which students learn by doing, including interactive, co-operative and participative forms of learning. Fourthly, a more open and collaborative relationship between teachers and learners is needed, replacing the traditional authoritarian model. Fifthly, it is necessary to set up new forms of co-operation and partnership between educational institutions and other actors and agents in society, such as parents, community organisations, local government, businesses, NGOs and foundations.

1.3. How does this compare with the American concept of "civic engagement"?

The concept and practice of education for democratic citizenship in the European context in many respects parallels civic education and civic engagement in the US context. Historically, American schools, colleges and universities have been held responsible for the development and maintenance of a democratic society through the preparation of an enlightened citizenry. In the 20th century, such efforts were often restricted to the provision of courses on government and national history or through volunteering. More recently a growing number of educational practitioners in the United States have argued that providing information about how a democracy works is not enough – civic skills must be internalised through practice. Citizenship is learned by experience when people come together to solve common problems and to discuss and listen to the views and concerns of others. There is also growing agreement that civic education must not be restricted to formal settings, but is a lifelong process involving formal and non-formal institutions in society.[8]

Like education for democratic citizenship, civic education tends to be used as an umbrella term for a number of different practices. However, while sharing the same basic sentiments and even some of the same language as the European approach, the American concept often has slightly different emphases. "Community engagement," or a responsibility to one's community, for example, has much greater prominence as an organising concept in the US approach than in Europe where the concepts of "democracy" and "human rights" are more usually found. The idea of community engagement in the US is often closely associated with civic outcomes in public rhetoric, that is, the idea that community involvement leads to the development of engaged citizens. In reality, however, the connection is often far more tenuous.

---

8. Kerr, D. and Nelson, J. (2006). "Active citizenship in INCA countries: definitions, policies, practices and outcomes." Final report. London: QCA/NFER.

Volunteer activities often fail to provide participants with a greater understanding of the underlying social and political factors that cause a problem in the first place. The term civic engagement has emerged in part because it underscores the importance of promoting political awareness and building democratic skills and values.

One of the most prevalent forms of civic engagement activity in the US is "service learning" – incorporating community-based activities into the formal curriculum. "Service learning" is predicated on the learning value of service to the local community or neighbourhood. In some instances, particular programmes also emphasise "character education" or the promotion of moral development through the teaching of virtues, such as justice, fairness, caring, respect, responsibility and trustworthiness, each in its own way seen as contributing to the creation of a more compassionate and responsible society. Such approaches are far more common in kindergarten through 12th grade settings than in higher education.

Efforts to promote community service, or "public service" as it was then known, in the late 1980s led to an increase in volunteering in US colleges and universities. In the 1990s a number of prominent initiatives were launched aimed at linking these activities with the core work of colleges and universities, namely teaching and research. Today, many, if not most, colleges and universities in the US offer courses with a "service-learning" component. In addition, hundreds of thousands of college students are also involved in outreach or volunteer efforts in their local communities annually. Such efforts have been encouraged by programmes instituted by the school system, beginning at the level of kindergarten and going through 12th grade (K-12). According to one 2008 study by the Corporation for National and Community Service, 68% of K-12 schools (and fully 86% of all high schools) offered opportunities for students to become involved in community service. Nearly a quarter of K-12 principals indicated that their schools offered credit bearing courses with a community-based learning component (service learning).[9] Higher education has witnessed a dramatic re-emphasis on civic engagement. Campus Compact, a coalition of college and university presidents committed to promoting civic engagement, has grown from three presidential members in 1985 to more than 1 100 in 2008, a quarter of all post-secondary institutions in the US. Its annual survey of members indicates that a third of all students at these institutions are involved in their communities as volunteers or in the context of service-learning courses for an average of five hours a week. Many campuses encourage faculty involvement.[10] Fully 85% of respondents to the survey indicated that they reward community-based research or service learning in faculty review, tenure, and/or promotions – a significant increase over the past five years.

Typically, however, the emphasis in service learning in the US has been largely on subject learning rather than democratic learning or outcomes.[11] The idea of

9. See www.nationalservice.gov/pdf/08_1112_lsa_prevalence.pdf.
10. See www.compact.org/about/statistics/.
11. Colby, A., Ehrlich, T., Beaumont, E. and Stephens, J. (2003), op. cit.; Hartley, M. and Soo, D. (2009), op.cit.

promoting democracy through such courses is a more recent emphasis. Similarly, despite a recent call for opportunities for young people to become more involved in leadership and decision making in service-learning programmes, there has been less emphasis on schools and universities as democratic communities in their own right and the need for more democratic forms of governance. The idea of a "holistic" approach and the need to identify school- and university-wide opportunities for the experience of democracy in action and to co-ordinate these with the formal curriculum, both in and across subjects, is much more rarely encountered in the US context.

Clearly, while they reflect different social and political priorities and concerns, European and US approaches have much to learn from each other – not least because neither Europe nor the US are homogenous entities, but are both made up of a plurality of communities each facing different problems and challenges. It is one of the aims of this publication to encourage this sharing process.

Chapter 2

School–community–university partnerships

2.1. What are EDC partnerships?

EDC partnerships are partnerships between organisations – such as national or regional ministries, local authorities, municipalities, NGOs, private foundations and formal and non-formal education organisations, including schools, colleges and institutions of higher education – which have as their primary purpose the aim of strengthening democracy in society, often through tackling a common problem. They are partnerships which are truly "civic" in the strict sense of the term, that is, relate to the rights and responsibilities of democratic citizenship. They aim both at building up the civic skills and dispositions of individuals and the democratic capital and resources of communities and societies as a whole at the same time as pursuing other specific goals.[12]

Recent interest in partnerships of this kind derives partly from the knowledge of the unique contributions that particular kinds of organisations are able to bring to democracy-building, and partly from an understanding of the complex and multi-dimensional task that democracy-building involves in a modern society.

In particular, partnerships between civil society organisations are able to take an "ecological", or "multilateral", approach to social change which cannot easily be achieved through the traditional "top-down", "technocratic" approach in which a small number of government or public authority "experts" attempt both to define and solve a problem unilaterally from outside. EDC partnerships can encourage the active participation of a wide range of different groups and bodies. They are able to recognise that communities are not monolithic entities but multilayered, rich in democratic potential waiting to be tapped. They can be both inclusive and reciprocal. They have the capacity to be effective at the grass-roots level whilst helping participants to see how their local context is linked to wider, regional, national and global issues and trends.

More fundamentally, EDC partnerships through their processes actually incorporate and bear witness to the democratic form of association. The contribution of each partner is defined and acknowledged. Their strengths and limitations are recognised and collaborative activities shaped carefully to take account of these. They understand, or should understand, each other's interests, even though these

---

12. See the Report on the Forum on Civic Partnerships of Citizenship and Human Rights Education (DGIV/EDU/CIT (2009) 12). Strasbourg: Council of Europe. Available at www.coe.int/edc.

may be different, whilst agreeing an overarching common purpose. In this way the contribution of each partner is clear and acknowledged, and common procedures for sharing information, making decisions and shaping programmes are developed and adjusted accordingly.

EDC partnerships can perhaps best be understood in the context of a continuum of co-operative efforts. There are different levels of partnership (see Table 1). On one end of this continuum is the simple exchange of information or goods between one organisation and another. A clothing drive at a local community centre that benefits a homeless shelter is an example of this kind of exchange. The next level of partnership involves dialogue, seeking to understand the interests and needs of each partner. Such dialogue may, over time, lead to the formation of networks – associations of individuals or representatives of groups that have shared interests. Some networks exist simply to share information or "best practices". Others may begin to take on common projects built around shared responsibilities. Such partnerships can lead to a shared sense of purpose – a common conviction that the partnership is engaged in important work that contributes to a common good. Partnerships that engage in such work, that build links across communities, that not only resolve specific problems but foster collective action to positively shape community life are EDC partnerships for sustainable democracy.

Table 1: Levels of partnership

Level of partnership	Types of activity	Example
Level 1: Exchange	Sharing information and/or materials	A group of university students approach several local school teachers about volunteering to read to children after school.
Level 2: Dialogue	Seeking to understand the interests and needs of each partner	The students invite faculty members who teach and conduct research on literacy to meet with the school teachers to learn more about the school and the community.
Level 3: Networking	Formation of associations with shared interests	The teachers, school administrators and faculty begin to devise projects aimed at improving the literacy of the children and providing experiential education opportunities for university students through several service-learning courses.
Level 4: Collaboration	Working together towards a common goal and, ideally, a common purpose	Over time, more teachers and faculty members begin to participate in meetings and additional projects emerge based on shared interests and goals.

Level of partnership	Types of activity	Example
Level 5: EDC partnering	Partnerships that address social problems and build democracy	Over time the project widens as other groups (community organisations and parent groups) become involved in defining the agenda of the partnership. Participants begin to raise questions about the larger socio-political causes of literacy problems in the community. The coalition works to gather information about these and begins to engage in collective action designed to amend public policy in this area

2.2. Why school–community–university partnering?

School–community–university partnering is only one possible type of EDC partnership among many. So what is special about school–community–university partnerships and what do they have to offer?

Schools and universities have long been recognised in both Europe and the United States as key vehicles for democratic development in society.

Schools are the community institutions par excellence, and situated at the heart of community life both physically and socially. It is at school that most people have their first experience of living and working in a civic institution. Schools are a common denominator in many people's lives, not only young people but adults, too, including teachers, parents, neighbours and community partners. They belong to all members of a community and are well suited to act as "hubs" around which local groups and activities can cohere. They are also well suited to act as catalysts for the solution of community problems, since many of the problems experienced in local communities – for example poverty, racism, religious and ethnic conflict, crime, drug abuse – are often also problems for their schools. The success of an in-school intervention at improving literacy among school students, for example, is likely to be significantly influenced, or even thwarted by factors from outside the school.

Universities are also situated at the heart of communities, particularly city communities, and have a similar capacity to contribute to community problem solving and civic renewal. In fact, it is becoming increasingly difficult for universities to ignore the social problems that exist immediately beyond the gates of their campuses. Not only do problems of this kind affect the recruitment and retention of university students and staff, but public and corporate funding is becoming more and more tied to social outcomes. Universities have access to human, technical and academic resources – essential in the identification and solution of community problems that are often not available elsewhere in society. Communities, in turn, can help universities to ground their academic work in everyday practical reality, making learning more relevant and helping to demolish the "ivory tower" mentality which is sometimes associated with higher education.

Schools together with institutions of higher education, therefore, form a "strategic subsystem"[13] in society, one which perhaps more than any other has the capacity to influence the functioning of society as a whole. There is thus huge potential in bringing the joint forces of schools and universities to bear alongside other groups and organisations in civil society to help citizens identify and solve the problems that exist in their communities: solutions are found to community problems; school and university students have opportunities to engage in "real-world" problem solving, enriching their educational development; schools and universities become more genuinely "civic" institutions; local communities become more involved in their own problem solving; and democratic values and practices are fostered across society.

Union of Roma Students in Vojvodina, Serbia

Roma are probably Europe's most downtrodden minority. They have been subject to entrenched harassment, discrimination and ghettoisation, supported in some cases by media characterisation of racist stereotypes, and frequently denied equal rights to education. In the Serbian autonomous province of Vojvodina, the Union of Roma Students is working together with schools and universities to improve access to higher education for young people of Roma origin. A project set up in 2008 is helping young Roma students to complete their secondary education through a programme of scholarships, guidance and counselling, thus motivating them to continue into higher education. Helping with access to higher education is an important element in the part universities can play in the promotion of democracy and human rights in society.[14]

However, with notable exceptions like the one above, we have yet to see the development of a substantial body of practice in this field either in Europe or in the United States. In the following sections, therefore, we look in more detail about what this kind of partnering might entail.

2.3. What makes a partnership an EDC one?

In seeking to encourage school–community–university partnerships in the context of the development of civic skills and attitudes and democratic capital in communities, it is important to distinguish partnerships of this kind from other reasons for school–university co-operation. There are many possible reasons for school–university co-operation, for example to facilitate teacher training or the teaching of

---

13. Harkavy, I. (1998), *School-Community-University Partnerships: Effectively Integrating Community Building and Educational Reform.* Conference paper, University of Pennsylvania.

14. The Roma Education Fund (www.romaeducationfund.hu/) oversees and supports many of the activities related to education of Roma, and many of these activities are now within the framework of the Decade of Roma Inclusion. The Council of Europe has also addressed this issue since 1969 and more systematically in the last 10 years through its Education of Roma Children programme and such bodies as the Roma and Travellers Forum. See www.coe.int/education/roma.

specific skills or specialist subjects, such as foreign languages in schools. Important though they may be, these cannot properly be described as EDC partnerships if the promotion of the civic capacity of individuals and of society is not prominent among their intended outcomes.

Similarly, there are school–community and university–community partnerships which are set up for specific purposes. Schools may wish to involve parents more closely in their children's education as a way of raising academic standards or improving pupil behaviour and attendance. University research departments may be involved in community projects geared towards the improvement of public health or transportation.

This is not to say that partnerships of these kinds do not contribute in any way to the democratic capacities of individuals and their communities, but that any contribution they make is likely to be incidental and unlikely to be sustained. School–community–university partnerships need to have the nurturing of democracy as a major aim if they are to function as EDC partnerships, as opposed to any other kind of social partnership.

Democracy building need not be the sole aim of a civic partnership, however: EDC partnerships can have a range of different aims and objectives. It seems likely that the most effective EDC partnerships are ones deriving from the need to solve wider community problems. Democracy is not built within a vacuum, but in real social environments with real people who have real interests and concerns. It is through the resolution of community issues and the solution of community problems that the civic skills and dispositions of individuals are enhanced and society is democratised.

This is shown clearly in the example of a school–university–community partnership from West Philadelphia. The partnership relied on multiple groups, each of which was vitally important in responding to the community need. The partnership began by developing a shared understanding of what the issue was and the goal that was being sought. The effort did far more than respond narrowly to a technical problem. It exemplified democratic action: it involved various members of a community from disparate organisations working together to advance meaningful change – changes in individual behaviour, curricular changes at the university and local schools, and changes in municipal policies about what constitutes safe housing. All of the partners were vitally important for this mutually supportive, reciprocal initiative.

Lead poisoning in West Philadelphia, Pennsylvania

Several years ago West Philadelphia parents became concerned about incidents of lead poisoning among young children. An existing partnership between administrators and faculty members at a local research university, a number of neighbourhood organisations and the local school system led to a series of efforts aimed at addressing the issue. Neighbourhood organisations called meetings in which individuals from all the partners came together to discuss the situation. Initiatives began to be developed.

Faculty members from the university's environmental studies programme and their students worked with pupils from the local schools to gather lab samples. Parents identified places where children tended to play. Local schoolteachers incorporated the project into the curriculum further raising awareness of the issue among their students (and by extension, their families) leading more children to become tested. Neighbourhood organisations spread word of the effort encouraging broader participation. They also invited members of the nursing faculty to parents meetings to discuss health problems associated with lead poisoning. The identification of areas with lead paint provided parents with the necessary information to lobby local officials and landlords to address the problem. The university faculty was able to gather data over time that demonstrated that the partners' work had made a positive difference.

What distinguishes EDC from other social partnerships, therefore, are both their goals and their methods, in particular the bringing together of multiple partners to define and find solutions to their own problems, in contrast to technocratic interventions where a group of outside "experts" come in, define the problem, formulate and implement a solution, then leave (see Table 2).

Table 2: EDC and non-EDC partnerships

EDC partnerships:	Non-EDC partnerships:
see communities as having assets and community members as critically important partners	see communities as having problems
believe that community members have their own knowledge, expertise and agency	believe that community members must be assisted
are inclusive and draw in many constituents to address systemic and complex challenges	are often limited in scope, and focus on discrete problems
are built on democratic principles – all partners shape the collective agenda	rely on a small group, special experts or officials to establish the agenda, often without consultation
allow the contributions of all partners to be defined, recognised and valued	value the expertise and interests of some partners more than others
exist not only to pursue specific goals but also to foster democratic principles and practices.	exist to address social problems.

2.4. What makes an EDC partnership a successful one?

Ultimately, one of the tests of a civic partnership of any kind is its effectiveness at supporting civic engagement and democratic citizenship at both an individual and a collective level. At the collective level, this can be "measured" in terms of the levels of civic participation in a community, and in the extent to which a community is able to manage issues of conflict and identify and provide solutions to its own problems. This in turn depends upon the levels of trust, reciprocity, co-operation, cohesion, shared understanding and communication and exchange. It also depends upon the creation of relationships, social networks and structures designed to support civic values and action.

The development of this kind of genuinely "civic" capacity at a collective level is intimately connected to the development of the same capacity within individuals. At the level of the individual participant, the effectiveness of EDC partnerships can be judged in terms of the presence of a range of civic and democratic characteristics or "competences" arising out of the partnership – from a sense of civic identity and responsibility to the development of sound practical judgment in relation to public policy making and implementation (see Table 3).

Table 3: Civic and democratic competences

Identity	Seeing oneself as a citizen, or member of society – feeling one belongs and has, or should have, equal rights, including the right and responsibility to participate civically and to make one's voice heard
Knowledge	Knowing about civic institutions and practices, and how they work
Awareness	Aware of the social issues, trends and problems current in one's community, and in society more generally
Skills	Able to access and interpret information relevant to community issues, to communicate, to argue a case and, where appropriate, take individual or collective action
Judgment	Able to evaluate the value and practicability of different policies, strategies and arrangements in the civic sphere.

Chapter 3

Making school–community–university partnerships work

3.1. How are EDC partnerships built?

What do school–community–university EDC partnerships look like? How does their work evolve and develop over time? How do they function? EDC partnerships range from simple to highly complex. Since EDC partnerships are a response by members of a community to pressing societal problems (or at least their manifestation locally) they can involve dozens, even hundreds of people. The precise mechanics of EDC partnerships vary and are influenced by a number of factors including the life cycle of the partnerships (early days may involve the participation of only a few individuals and draw in others as the effort expands and matures), the number of partner organisations and the scope of the projects being undertaken.

The most basic partnership consists of two individuals who find they have common interests or concerns and decide to collaborate. Yet even a simple arrangement such as this requires that goals be set, a division of labour be devised, the preferred means of communication identified, and a process for evaluation and self-correction established. When partnerships are complex, involving multiple partners, it is even more important to establish these structures and group norms to ensure the ongoing health of the effort.

Regardless of size and scope, effective EDC partnerships require careful attention to both structures (the development of organisational procedures, policies about how the partnership makes decisions and will carry out its work) and group norms and dynamics (a shared understanding of why the group is together, shared goals, and the cultivation of openness and trust). Partners must be committed to making a concerted effort to ensure that both the structure of the partnership and a common and equitable sense of meaningful work are cultivated and maintained.

Partnerships are dynamic entities. A nascent partnership often emerges from simple activities. These may include the sharing of information or resources or participating in a modest short-term project. Such opportunities give prospective partners the opportunity to learn more about each other which may reveal shared interests and goals. This, in turn, can lead to additional more sustained joint action on other projects. Over time what might begin as a simple transactional exchange can blossom into a committed, mutually beneficial partnership based on democratic principles.

The development of an EDC partnership can be viewed in terms of three consecutive stages (see Table 4).

3.1.1. Formation

The origins of civic partnerships can be found in dialogue between prospective partners. This may reveal that there is a convergence of interests in addressing a pressing societal challenge or need. A first step towards a partnership is identifying possible stakeholders and beginning the process of engaging in dialogue about their interests and goals. What do they care about? What do they hope to achieve? What are the inherent strengths of the various partners? What are their constraints? What particular skills and expertise do they have? How can these be combined to produce meaningful change around the established goal(s)?

3.1.2. Growth

Once common goals are identified it is important to begin to establish certain procedures and processes for planning. The partnership may develop layers of involvement for different kinds of participants. Although an EDC partnership is built on the notion that the voices of all participants are valuable and important, complex or specialised partnership activities may involve many subsets of people. A whole variety of arrangements may be developed by which broad-based consultation for key decisions may be sought while certain operational decision making can be undertaken by representatives of relevant partners.

3.1.3. Self-evaluation and refinement

It is also important to establish procedures for periodic review of the projects being undertaken by the partners. Are they functioning smoothly? Are there adjustments that need to be made? Are the projects a good use of collective time and energy? It is important periodically to revisit the purpose of the partnership. Is it achieving its overarching goal? Might the collective energy of the partnership be allocated in other ways? Finally, it is also important periodically to discuss whether each of the partners are satisfied with the rewards of the partnership relative to their contributed efforts. Is the distribution of work equitable (or is there a compelling reason why this is not the case)? Have the priorities of any of the partners changed to such a degree that it might be best if they left the partnership? Are there others who might be approached about joining the partnership's efforts? Has the partnership achieved what it set out to achieve, or has it reached the end of its natural life and needs to be dissolved? Do new forms of partnership need to be considered?

Table 4: The structural and normative dimensions of building a partnership

	Structural elements	Group norms and dynamics
Stage 1: Formation	identification of potential partners	dialogue that reveals shared goals
	calling joint meetings	beginning to learn about the other (their priorities, hopes, strengths, limitations)
	brainstorming	
	planning potential projects	establishing norms of transparency
		ensuring all partners have a voice
Stage 2: Growth	establishing appropriate structures for decision making	continually affirming shared goals
	defining responsibilities based on the interests, strengths and limitations of the various partners	articulating and appreciating the unique contributions of each partner
	identifying additional needs and other potential partners	amending decision-making processes as project and pro-grammes proliferate
		ensuring all partners feel that they have influence over the partnership's agenda
Stage 3: Self-evaluation and refinement	periodically reviewing the decision-making procedures and adjusting as necessary	revising the projects and ask-ing whether they are the best means of realising the partner-ship's goals
	re-evaluating the division of labour based on the current strengths and constraints of the partners	discussing if there are other ways for the partnership to expend its energies
	dissolving the partnership when it has achieved what it set out to achieve, or reached the end of its natural life	openly discussing how satis-fied the partners are with the arrangement, and how well their needs are being met
	considering new forms of partnership	considering whether there are partners whose priorities have changed or who have grown apart from the rest of the partners?

3.2. What are the challenges to EDC partnerships and how can they be met?

Despite their many advantages and potential rewards, it is also important to note that school–community–university partnerships can be immensely challenging undertakings. Their enduring success requires the cultivation of mutual understanding, the development of appropriate decision-making processes, the identification of shared goals (and transparency about outcomes that are likely to benefit one partner over others). It also entails recognising that while each partner is a valuable contributor to an initiative's overall success, there may be disparities in the power and influence that must be accounted for. Each of the above issues represents an area where mismanagement or inattention can threaten the partnership. There are key questions that need to be asked (see Table 5).

3.2.1. Knowing the other

Individuals and groups may be drawn to partnerships for a variety of reasons. A strong EDC partnership rests on the firm foundation of mutual understanding. Each of the partners must take time to learn about the core work of the other partners. What are their most pressing priorities? What are the expectations they labour under in their roles? This is a step that is often skipped in the interests of formulating an action agenda. It can be a mistake. EDC partnerships, by definition, draw together different individuals and groups to address pressing real-world problems. While the various partners will have shared interests, there are also aspects of their work that constitute competing or even contradictory commitments. For example, a community partner may wonder why a university faculty member seems resistant to volunteering more time at the project site. The faculty member, on the other hand, may be mystified by the fact that the community partner does not appreciate all the time she is spending devising a research protocol that will test the efficacy of the intervention. The community member needs volunteers. The university expects that faculty member to produce research. Such misunderstandings can become invisible stumbling blocks. The remedy is greater awareness of the constraints that the other partners are working under.

3.2.2. Transparency regarding outcomes

As partners begin imagining how they might work together, it is important to define the desired outcomes of each of the partners. Some goals will be shared. Others, however, may be of interest to only one. For example, a group of school teachers, the staff from a local community centre and faculty members from a university may all have a keen interest in promoting the arts. The school teachers may be interested in finding ways to weave the arts into the school's curriculum. The community centre's director may want to expand the use of its facility and serve the entire community. Members of the faculty may be interested in providing graduate students with teaching experience. Discussing these interests is another way of understanding the competing demands on the various partners. That may lead to a measure of accommodation around how various duties are assigned. For example, the community centre director may be generally supportive but not have the time to actively participate in the evaluation research conducted by the faculty member.

Such discussions also reveal opportunities to collaborate that were not evident before. The school teachers may find that, because of official curriculum require-ments, fitting additional arts programming into the school day is difficult. On the other hand, an after-school programme at the community centre might be developed that makes connections with ideas being taught in classes. Furthermore, students from the university might then work with the teachers to devise and deliver an after-school arts curriculum. A partnership built on open communication has the best chance of evolving into a mutually supportive EDC partnership that benefits the community, society and all of the partners. Without this level of transparency, partners may become confused or arrive at misconceptions about the level of com-mitment of various partners.

3.3.3. Accounting for disparities in power

While all partners make a contribution to a partnership, their efforts and level of interest are rarely perfectly symmetrical. Some partners may have only a small (though important) stake in the overall enterprise. Others may see it as a significant element of their work. As discussed above, partners may have outcomes that are primarily of interest to them and not the other partners. Partnerships also often have disparities in power and influence. Most community-based organisations in the United States rely on volunteers to provide their programmes and many must struggle to find external funding (from foundations or private sources). Being offered the opportunity to partner with a relatively resource-rich university could create a dynamic in which the community partner feels unable to say "no" to the university partner for fear of losing those resources. However, all partners have something valuable to offer any initiative. Although the resources of one may be greater, each is needed to advance the shared goal. One strategy for mitigating the deleterious aspects of relationships where there is uneven power is to spell out clearly the contributions that each partner is making. A healthy sign of any partnership is when all partners have to adapt their plans or make concessions for the project to move forward. This ensures that no single partner is dominating.

Table 5: Key questions

Key questions:
Do all partners have a say in fashioning the agenda of the partnership and influ-encing activities in which they participate?
Does each partner have a rich understanding of the overall work being undertaken by the others?

Are the strengths of and the constraints upon each partner understood?

Are the contributions of each partner clear?

Is the benefit to each partner clearly articulated?

Have the partners openly discussed any disparities in power that might exist in the partnership?

Are all partners committed to negotiating differences in opinions and confronting and resolving potential conflict between themselves?

Are the activities of the partnership regularly monitored and evaluated?

Is the partnership adjusting and growing as it evolves over time, for example as new people enter, others leave and goals shift?

Is the partnership continuing to serve the interests and needs of all the partners?

Chapter 4

School–university–community partnerships in practice

Case study 1: Refugee Support Network, Leeds, United Kingdom

Leeds University is at the forefront of community engagement in the UK, being one of the first to develop a community relations strategy, employ a full-time community liaison officer and develop a community-sensitive housing strategy. The outcome of this approach is a consultative and engaging university which is both proactive and responsive to the needs identified within the local community.

The university believes that the appointment of a dedicated community liaison officer has been crucial in forging new relationships and partnerships with the local community. Increased awareness of this role through sustained and regular attendance of local group meetings presents the university as a listening and lasting presence. Previously, community relations principally involved reacting to issues, often as a result of conflict generated in areas of local residents and transient student populations. This remains a core function of the role, and dealing with issues and complaints is managed through a dedicated neighbourhood helpline.

The role is also proactive, seeking to develop projects within the community to utilise the student resource as a benefit to local people and devise, in consultation with the community, new and innovative strategies to prevent recurring problems. Working in this way has enabled the community to feel a sense of ownership and to give a direction to projects, and has in all cases improved perceptions of the university. It is clear that building links with the community involves engagement in not only social events but also in consultation on policy matters that can affect the locality.

During the academic year 2002-03 the university became involved in the Refugee Support Network (RSN), a self-help group set up by primary and secondary school teachers working with pupils whose first language is not English. The pupils come from different backgrounds, most being children of asylum seekers and refugees, others moving to the UK because of their parents' work, but all have immediate need of language support. The university is well placed to support such a demand due to the large numbers of international and language students.

The Refugee Support Network has been extremely successful in recruiting previously low participating or non-participating volunteers. It has attracted a much higher percentage of international students (over 50%) and postgraduates (25%) than any of the university's other 15 volunteering programmes (5% and 3% respectively).

International students clearly see an opportunity to offer support using their first language. They often cite a lack of confidence in their own English as a barrier to volunteering on other projects. There is also an affinity and a desire to assist people that speak their own first language who have faced and continue to face deprivation and disadvantage.

The Refugee Support Network is delivered in a uniquely flexible and responsive way to take account of the changing situations and circumstances of the refugee and asylum-seeker population. Typically, refugee and asylum-seeker families are transient, often having to move to different homes and schools. They are also mainly housed in low demand social housing predominantly in areas of significant deprivation in the inner city. This situation is detrimental to planning; indeed, schools are not able to predict or plan when new pupils will arrive. Volunteers are therefore informed of these circumstances and are made aware that completing a placement may involve changing schools with the children or ending the support if the child is relocated out of the city.

Volunteers assist young people to assimilate in the classroom, improve their English and raise their confidence. They have also on occasions helped schools with translation and interpretation between the teachers and the parents. Children in some circumstances have better English language skills than their parents, and parents have used the support to ask questions about many other aspects of their lives.

Requests for languages continue to grow exponentially and each request is logged on a database. Equally volunteers may come forward with a particular first language that has not been requested. In seeking to meet the demands for the many languages, volunteers have been recruited through personal contacts, student societies and even contacts from other universities and organisations.

To date the RSN has placed over 100 volunteers in local schools. Requests for languages include Portuguese, Arabic, French, Swahili, Afrikaans, Cantonese, Mandarin, Kurdish, Russian and Czech. Registered volunteers include those from the Philippines, Slovakia, Iran, Brazil and Russia. Student societies are naturally an excellent source of potential volunteers, with many groups formed on the basis of nationality.

This is a unique school–community–university project that has caught the hearts and minds of many new student volunteers who would not otherwise have been involved in a community engagement programme, helping them to become aware of aspects of civic life previously unknown to them and to develop a strong sense of civic agency. It assists local schools in the assimilation of young refugees and asylum seekers, improving their facility in English, building their sense of civic identity and belonging in the local community, and promoting a culture of democracy and human rights.

Adapted from: www.leeds.ac.uk/ace/awards/refugee.html

Case study 2: University-assisted community schools, Pennsylvania, United States of America

An example of school–community–university partnering from the United States that is consonant with the civic partnership ideal is the university-assisted community school (UACS). The partnership is predicated on the idea that partnerships must be built on inclusive, democratic processes and that a key outcome of the partnership must be promoting the community voice and encouraging participatory democracy. A central tenet of the UACS model is that effective education can only exist in a healthy, supportive and active community environment. As many have observed, schools are well positioned to serve as hubs for community building. When they fill this role, they can foster decentralised, democratic, community-based responses to significant community problems. This approach has gained considerable support in the US over the past decade. The Coalition for Community Schools, an association that supports such efforts, has grown from five partner organisations in 1997 to more than 170 today and its members include major education, youth development, family support and community development organisations.

The following account details how one of these partnerships evolved. The University of Pennsylvania (Penn) established a centre to encourage and support partnerships with the community in 1992. From the beginning of these efforts community leaders had made clear that health care was a critically important community issue. A number of small initiatives were launched with various degrees of success. However, in the spring of 2002 a group of undergraduates enrolled on a course that emphasised community-based problem solving chose to focus their research on the health-care crisis in the community. Their research led them to propose the creation of a health promotion and disease prevention centre at an area school, specifically the Sayre Middle School with whom the university had already worked. They argued that for a school-based community health-care project to be sustained, it would have to be integrated into the curriculum at both the university and the state school. Only then would it gain a measure of stability. They envisioned the creation of a health promotion/disease prevention centre at a local school that would serve as a teaching and learning focus for medical, dental, nursing, arts and sciences, social work, education, fine arts and business students.

The students' report spurred a number of discussions with administrators and faculty at the university and professionals at the Sayre School who began meeting to discuss the feasibility of establishing such a school-based health centre. (It is worth noting that one of the undergraduates who developed the Sayre project, Mei Elansary, received the 2003 Howard R. Swearer Humanitarian Award given by Campus Compact to students for outstanding public service.) Faculty members from Medicine, Nursing, Dentistry, Social Work, Arts and Sciences, Fine Arts, and Education eventually became involved in the effort, developing new courses, and reshaping existing courses and internships and research projects to support the initiative.

The Community Health Promotion and Disease Prevention Centre at Sayre Middle School was formally launched in January 2003. It functions as the central component of a university-assisted community school, designed both to advance student learning and to help strengthen families and institutions within the community. Sayre students have become agents of health-care change in their neighbourhoods. They are not passive recipients of health information. Rather, they are active deliverers of information and co-ordination and creative providers of service. The school has become a locus for community organising activities. Sayre is not just where students go to learn during the day, it is also where community members gather. Moreover, the multidisciplinary character of the Sayre Health Promotion and Disease Prevention Centre enables it to be integrated into the curriculum and co-curriculum of both the state school and the university, assuring an educational focus as well as sustainability for the Sayre centre. In fact, the core of the programme is to integrate the activities of the Sayre centre with the educational programmes and curricula at both Sayre Middle School and Penn.

The partnership continues to evolve. On the university side, the University of Pennsylvania's Netter Center for Community Partnerships helps build bridges between the university faculty and the school, and its staff members help co-ordinate meetings and ensure goals are being met. Dr Bernette Johnson, Senior Medical Officer and Associate Dean of Community Outreach and Diversity for Penn's medical school established a committee of faculty members involved in the partnership. The committee is beginning to define specific issues (for example college access) that might tie the initiatives of multiple faculty members together. It is also designing an evaluation programme in order to better gauge the impact of existing programmes. Staff members from the centre meet with teachers and administrators at the school regularly to engage in troubleshooting. Although there is no Sayre staff member wholly dedicated to supporting the partnership, a number of Sayre teachers and staff members have been involved in the project on an ongoing basis. (Like many urban schools, Sayre has experienced turnover in its teaching staff and school leadership and had to navigate shifts in district priorities.) Recently the district has considered changing Sayre's status from a neighbourhood school to a magnet school that would draw from across the city, which would have implications for how the "community" being served by the school is defined. The sustainability of the partnership is dependent upon flexibility and communication in order to ensure the needs of all partners are met.

Currently, hundreds of Penn students (professional, graduate and undergraduate) and dozens of faculty members, from a wide range of Penn schools and departments, work at Sayre. The participants in these efforts are simultaneously involved in academic research, teaching and learning. They are practising specialised skills and developing, in important ways, their moral and civic consciousness and democratic character. And since they are engaged in a highly integrated common project, they are also learning how to communicate, interact and collaborate with each other in wholly unprecedented ways that have measurably broadened their academic horizons and demonstrated to them the real value of working to overcome disciplinary tribalism. At Penn, successful concrete real-world problem solving has spoken louder and more convincingly than abstract exhortation.

Appendix I

Education for democratic citizenship (EDC) and human rights education (HRE) – a definition

Education for democratic citizenship (EDC) and human rights education (HRE) are defined by the Council of Europe as follows:

"Education for democratic citizenship" means education, training, dissemination, information, practices and activities which aim, by equipping learners with knowledge, skills and understanding and developing their attitudes and behaviour, to empower them to exercise and defend their democratic rights and responsibilities in society, to value diversity and to play an active part in democratic life, with a view to the promotion and protection of democracy and the rule of law.

"Human rights education" means education, training, dissemination, information, practices and activities which aim, by equipping learners with knowledge, skills and understanding and developing their attitudes and behaviour, to empower them to contribute to the building and defence of a universal culture of human rights in society, with a view to the promotion and protection of human rights and fundamental freedoms.

Education for democratic citizenship and human rights education are closely interrelated and mutually supportive. They differ in focus and scope rather than in goals and practices. Education for democratic citizenship focuses primarily on democratic rights and responsibilities and active participation, in relation to the civic, political, social, economic, legal and cultural spheres of society, while human rights education is concerned with the broader spectrum of human rights and fundamental freedoms in every aspect of people's lives.[15]

---

15. See: www.coe.int/edc.

Appendix II

EDC partnerships – recommendations of the 2008 forum

On 9 and 10 October 2008 a Forum on Civic Partnerships for Citizenship and Human Rights Education[16] was organised by the Council of Europe in Strasbourg within the framework of the Swedish Presidency of the Committee of Ministers.

The aim of the forum was to produce recommendations on how civic partnerships supporting EDC could be developed and supported at a national and European level and it included an exploration of different understandings and experiences of EDC partnerships and an exchange of examples of good practice.

Participants included officials from the states parties to the European Cultural Convention, representatives of international institutions and civil society, and foundations active in the field of EDC. Member states were each asked to nominate a high-ranking official dealing with citizenship and human rights education, and Council of Europe EDC/HRE co-ordinators were asked to recommend one prominent representative of civil society active in EDC/HRE in their respective countries.

The following three extracts are reproduced from the forum report.[17]

Extract 1: The essential characteristics of civic partnerships

> While there was unanimous agreement among the participants about the value of partnership working in the creation of more effective citizenship and human rights education, it was felt important to avoid a too narrow concept of what this might mean in practice, both in terms of the kind of organisations involved and the nature of the relationship. It is difficult to arrive at a set of common criteria and recommendations because each case is unique. Educational systems and civil society organisations are different from one country, region, canton or municipality to another and opportunities for partnership working vary from one situation to the next. In some situations the role of NGOs and other civil society organisations in EDC/HRE is highly developed, whereas in others it is just beginning to get under way. However, although there are important lessons to be learned from the experience of the former, we must not make the mistake of thinking that there is only one model for civic partnerships in this field or that the same process of development should be followed.

> While there may be no ideal model of a partnership working in EDC/HRE, participants agreed, however, that at a generic level there are some common features that distinguish these kinds of partnerships from others:

---

16. In recognition of the essential relationship between human rights and democratic citizenship, Council of Europe documents usually refer to "Education for democratic citizenship and human rights education (EDC/HRE)" – see Appendix 1.

17. Council of Europe (2009), Report on the Forum on Civic Partnerships for Citizenship and Human Rights Education, Strasbourg, DGIV/EDU/CIT 12.

1. Civic partnerships in EDC/HRE exist to solve problems

The reason for the partners coming together in the first place is to solve a particular kind of problem. The problem can take different forms. It may be a need to be satisfied, for example a lack of appropriate teacher training in EDC/HRE, or perhaps a request to be fulfilled, for instance schools asking for help on how to deal with controversial issues in the classroom. It is the nature of the problem that determines the type of partners that should come together, their respective roles and working methods.

2. Civic partnerships in EDC/HRE exist to solve problems and promote EDC/HRE

The problem a civic partnership in EDC/HRE exists to solve is always an educational one – specifically, one relating to citizenship or human rights education. The outcome, if the partnership is successful, will be an improvement in some aspect of EDC/HRE. Of course, other sorts of problem – for example practical or political – may need to be solved along the way, but these will always be secondary to the EDC/HRE purpose.

3. Civic partnerships in EDC/HRE exist to solve problems that cannot be solved by the state alone

The reason the partnership is needed is that the problem it exists to solve, for whatever reason, cannot be solved by the state alone. It may be that the state doesn't have the necessary resources, human or financial, at the time or it may be a problem that as a matter of principle the state ought not to be left to deal with on its own.

4. The ultimate beneficiaries of civic partnerships in EDC/HRE are the citizens and residents of Europe

The ultimate beneficiaries of the process are the citizens and residents of Europe. They may benefit directly through what might be called "primary" partnerships, that is, ones organised to deliver immediate learning, or indirectly, through "secondary" partnerships, that is, ones organised for capacity building for this purpose. The parties that come together in partnership may have something to gain from the process as well, of course. In fact, the prospect of mutual benefit may be a powerful incentive for the formation of partnerships in the first place, but the EDC/HRE outcome will always have priority.

Extract 2: The benefits of civil society involvement

In discussing the role of civil society in EDC/HRE, participants identified a number of definite benefits that civil society organisations can bring to partnership working with public authorities, including:

1. Grass-roots working

Civil society organisations are often better equipped to work at the grass-roots level with individual schools and communities. EDC/HRE begins on the ground with actual schools and communities. "Bottom-up" working of the type carried out in small local projects is the only way in which the frequently mentioned "compliance gap" between policy and practice may be overcome in this field. Citizens at grass-roots level are often suspicious of state initiatives and put more trust in locally based organisations. Indeed there are some EDC/HRE problems that can only be solved at the local level. An example given of a partnership designed with exactly this in mind is the One Square Kilometre project in Germany which brings together all local stakeholders around a local school with staff from an NGO doing some of the teaching. This project is now being carried out in over ten different schools.

2. Flexibility

Smaller civil society organisations are often more flexible that departments of state. They also tend to be able to bring more energy and enthusiasm to bear than slow-moving state bureaucracies.

3. Experiment and innovation

On account of freedom from state control, civil society organisations have the potential to be more experimental in their approach, developing and trying out new concepts and ways of working in EDC/HRE, which if successful can then be taken up by the public authorities on a wider scale. In this respect they can act as catalysts for innovation and new developments in EDC/HRE.

4. Expertise

Civil society organisations often have specialist expertise in aspects of citizenship and human rights education which is not readily available elsewhere, for example in EDC/HRE pedagogy, curriculum development, resource production and training. NGOs are by their nature specialist organisations with relatively specific aims and methods and can have much to offer the state in terms of partnership working on this account, particularly with regard to current issues and problems in society. An example was given of a local NGO in Bulgaria developing teaching on trafficking through the Compass HRE manual – a problem which schools were finding difficulty in dealing with. International organisations often have their own particular areas of expertise to offer, for example translation of materials or knowledge of best practice internationally. Many different kinds of "know-how" are required for EDC/HRE and this underlines the need for partnership working in this field, bringing together academics as well as advocates and activists.

Participants cited a wide range of examples of this, for instance, the partnership between the Serbian Ministry of Education and the NGO Civic Initiatives in the preparation of textbooks, capacity building for teachers, competitions and the publication of a practical magazine on civic education for teachers. Another example is the Armenian Human Rights School set up by a local NGO in collaboration with the Ministry of Education and Science to train teachers in legal education, including human rights and national law – a subject new to schools in the country. With funding from donor organisations, including from the Netherlands, NGO staff help teachers work towards a professional certificate qualifying them to teach this subject in school.

5. A systematic and coherent approach

Civil society organisations are often better equipped to promote a more systematic approach to EDC/HRE than public authorities. This can be especially important in situations where a decentralised system of education results in different attitudes and approaches to EDC/HRE being adopted in different schools or regions within a country. Coming from civil society themselves, civic partners tend to be better placed to help schools approach EDC/HRE in a more holistic way, linking civic education as a classroom subject with democratic governance within the school community and experiential learning in the wider community beyond the school gates, for example by facilitating local "hands-on" projects. The implications of a whole-school approach to EDC/HRE learning are not yet always fully understood and there is much that civil society can do to develop and disseminate good practice in this field, for example by developing national standards or guidelines. As an example of this, School Councils UK, a UK NGO, is currently working on national standards for school councils.

6. Continuity

Civil society organisations are often able to take a more long-term view to EDC/HRE development than state bodies and thus help to create more sustainable arrangements and ways of working in schools. In the absence of support from civic partners, state-promoted EDC/HRE can be highly dependent on the political agenda of the government of the time. Changes in government or in education personnel often lead to changes of educational direction. Through partnership working with the state, civil society organisations are able to create forms of EDC/HRE learning that have more permanence and are more able to withstand changes of political climate or official personnel, for example through long-term agreements or protocols, or the establishment of periodic events, such as annual competitions, or "citizenship" or "human rights" days.

7. Alternative sources of funding

Civil society organisations often have access to sources of funding not available to the state, for example from private foundations, individual philanthropy, corporate sponsorship or marketing. In situations where this is the case, civil society organisa-tions are able to give financial support to developments in EDC/HRE at a national level or make up for disparities in state funding across a country, for instance in Italy where the north of the country receives more state funding than the south. This can range from anything from funding the development and trialling of new projects to the supply of training, resources or other technical services to teachers and schools free of charge.

8. "Watchdog" status

Civil society organisations are in the unique position of being able to hold governments to account over policy development and implementation in EDC/HRE. In the view of some participants at the forum, this is one of the most valuable contributions that civic partners can bring to partnership working. Civic partners are able to remind the state of its obligations, for example to the European Convention on Human Rights, and to work to prevent EDC/HRE from becoming political propaganda. Civic partners have the capacity to act as "correcting" agents monitoring government action in this field, in particular, with regard to transparency, accountability and financial management. They are able to bring a measure of congruence to what central and local government says about citizenship and human rights education, what parents and other "stakeholders" understand and want from the process and the kind of teaching and learning experi-ences that go on in schools and other forms of education. The example was quoted of the development of partnership working between parents and teachers through the creation of school councils in Georgian schools. These councils draw together differ-ent local stakeholders to discuss the distribution of funding and school development, including the election of principals, bringing much needed transparency and account-ability to a public service where there were previously many allegations of financial mismanagement.

9. Trust

Finally, civic partners are able to overcome some of the current disillusionment with public life and institutions by making society more accessible to the citizen and creating more opportunities for citizen participation in society – both at a national and a European level. They are able to begin to build up an atmosphere of trust in social institutions and services – particularly important at a time of financial crisis – and a more "ethical" approach to public life.

Extract 3: Criteria for effective civic partnerships

The identification of success criteria for civic partnerships in EDC/HRE was one of the central tasks of the forum and stimulated much discussion. Although there was some difficulty in generalising given the wide range of organisations covered and the possible ways in which they might work together – there being no one model of a good civic partnership as such – there was substantial agreement among participants about some of the basic features essential to any civic partnership to be an effective one, including:

1. A common objective

While effective civic partnerships in EDC/HRE do not necessarily depend upon partners sharing the same interests or values, or even general goals, what they do need to share is a common objective for the partnership, that is, the problem they are coming together to solve (although it can only be possible if partners are aware of and discuss their differences as well as their commonalities). It means a measure of agreement about the aspect of EDC/HRE it is intended to improve, the means to improve it and an acceptance that this may only be achieved, or best achieved, through joint working. The objective should be specified as clearly as possible so that each partner knows exactly what it is they are involved in. It should be realistic and, as far as possible, evidence-based, in other words rooted in up-to-date research on teaching and learning, and young peoples' understanding and experience of life in contemporary Europe.

How the objective is first identified and by whom is unimportant. It may come from any number of different sources, for example from a public enquiry, an NGO, a school or even a group of school students. Who initiates the idea of partnership in the first place is also unimportant; it is the outcome that counts.

2. Clearly defined roles

It is essential that partners have a clear understanding of what the individual contribution of each is intended to be and that there is joint agreement on this. All of the partners should approve their respective roles. This is not to say that precise roles have to be decided at the outset, however. Identifying and refining roles is likely to involve a process of negotiation over time, demanding a certain amount of flexibility and open-mindedness, and mutual respect between the partners. The roles may be very different, but they should be complimentary – this is the point of the partnership. It is also better if it involves a range of key personnel in the organisations, not just a few select individuals. An example illustrating this clear division of labour was cited from Belgium where about ten years ago the Ministry of Education established a new structure for publicising NGO services to schools, in which the offers made by NGOs are co-ordinated and subjected to quality control by the ministry.

3. Equality

While it might be unreasonable to expect partners to be equal in every respect, for example in terms of size, access to funding, or political power (one could hardly expect a civil society to have the same power as the state), the idea that partners should be able to discuss their joint objectives and working methods as equal "interlocutors" had much more support from participants. The importance of each partner retaining their integrity of purpose was emphasised.

This will not only have the effect of leading to better decision making and more effective action, but will also allow for the proper balance between state and civil society actors in matters of democratic education, in particular, the safeguarding of the autonomy and "critical" function of civil society vis-à-vis the state.

It will also allow partnership working to become an exercise in democracy and human rights in its own right. A number of participants argued for the importance of gender equality in EDC/HRE partnership working, given that women in many European countries still do not have equal opportunities of participation in public life. Others argued for the importance of involving children and young people in developing agendas for partnership working and having a chance to express their own opinions. Achieving this would require the development of an explicit culture of dialogue between partners and a climate of trust and mutual respect.

4. Openness and accountability

The quality of openness was recognised as important for EDC/HRE partnerships, namely, openness both between partners and between partners and the wider public. Partners need to be able to work openly with each other in specifying objectives, planning their activities and so on. They also need to communicate what they are trying to achieve to the range of stakeholders that have an interest in their activities, including parents and other community members, officials and elected representatives. For a number of participants this suggested a greater role for the media (including television and popular websites), as well as modern ICT tools (such as skype, e-learning platforms, etc.) in partnerships. Not only would this give partnerships greater visibility, but it would also build in a greater element of public accountability, both through informing and potentially through involving key stakeholders in EDC/HRE, for example the parents of school students. EDC/HRE should be open and accountable in a general sense to the society within which they are working.

5. Sustainability

A key feature of effective EDC/HRE partnerships was thought to be the extent to which they are able to lead to educational practices that are sustainable. While a certain amount of stability is required if civic partnerships are to effect permanent changes in this way, it is not necessary that the partnership itself is sustainable in the long run. What is more important is that the practices which it establishes are sustainable. Partnerships should not be judged in terms of their short-term successes but rather in terms of what happens after the partnership ends. Will what has been gained be immediately lost, or will it continue and grow? Partner organisations need to take a long-term view of what makes for more effective citizenship and human rights education in the countries in which they are operating and plan their activities in the light of this. One way to build in sustainability is to create partnerships capable of making a structural difference to the education system, for example through developing standards and qualifications, professional development accreditation and certification, or quality assurance mechanisms. An interesting example from Romania was quoted of a joint NGO-government round table that was set up to deal with a problem concerning the adoption of children; the problem was solved but the round table still exists.

6. Evaluation and self-evaluation

Regular reflection on progress was thought to be another essential feature of an effective partnership. While summative evaluation can provide valuable information on which to bid for or plan future projects and partnerships, formative evaluation – particularly self-evaluation – is more able to ensure that the desired outcomes of the partnership are achieved.

Appendix III

The Council of Europe and the Democratic Citizenship and Human Rights Education project

The Council of Europe is Europe's oldest institution, with 47 member states. Its core values and priorities are human rights, democracy and the rule of law. It is considered a leader organisation in the field of democratic citizenship and human rights education. The Council of Europe's flagship project, Democratic Citizenship and Human Rights Education, started in 1997 and is currently in its fourth phase. Through this programme, the Council of Europe has adopted reference texts, developed political frameworks, supported networks and forums and produced high quality materials in the area of citizenship and human rights education.

1. Political framework

The following recommendations have been agreed upon by all member states through either the executive body of the Council of Europe, the Committee of Ministers (representatives of ministries of foreign affairs) or the Parliamentary Assembly of the Council of Europe:

–   Recommendation 1849 (2008) of the Parliamentary Assembly for the promotion of a culture of democracy and human rights through teacher education;

–   Recommendation Rec(2002)12 of the Committee of Ministers to member states on education for democratic citizenship (this recommendation was translated by the European Commission into the languages of all EU states);

–   Recommendation 1346 (1997) of the Parliamentary Assembly on human rights education;

–   Council of Europe Charter on Education for Democratic Citizenship and Human Rights Education adopted in the framework of Recommendation CM/Rec(2010)7 of the Committee of Ministers. This framework policy document will be an important reference point for all of Europe and will be used as a basis for the Council of Europe's future work in this field in the coming years.

2. Networking and forums

The Council of Europe supports a network of EDC/HRE co-ordinators appointed by the ministries of education. These co-ordinators meet twice a year and are a major contributor to both the Organisation's work, on the one hand, and implementation within member states on the other. Many of the co-ordinators are currently working on reforms in their countries regarding EDC/HRE, or have recently been involved in preparing and implementing such reforms.

In addition, the Council of Europe supports regional networks on EDC/HRE, including a South-Eastern Europe EDC/HRE Network that meets twice a year.

The Council of Europe also organises regular forums to bring together large numbers of key stakeholders on EDC/HRE issues, including NGOs active in this field. The last one was held in Strasbourg in October 2008 and was entitled: Civic Partnerships for Citizenship and Human Rights Education. In this context many experts from the NGO side also work with the Directorate General of Education, Culture and Heritage, Youth and Sport of the Council of Europe.

3. Materials

The Council of Europe has produced a wealth of materials. The major ones, called the "EDC/HRE Pack" are the following:

Tool 1: *Policy Tool for EDC/HRE: Strategic Support for Decision Makers*

Tool 2: *Democratic Governance of Schools*

Tool 3: *How All Teachers can support Citizenship and Human Rights Education: A Framework for the Development of Competences*

Tool 4: *Quality Assurance of Education for Democratic Citizenship in Schools*

Tool 5: *School-Community-University Partnerships for a Sustainable Democracy: Education for Democratic Citizenship in Europe and the United States of America*

These instruments have been negotiated and approved by a large number of experts from all member states, including the EDC/HRE co-ordinators.

In addition, a host of supplementary materials can be found on the Organisation's website (www.coe.int/edc).

A series of high quality materials for teachers for use in the classroom in the field of EDC/HRE were recently produced, including:

– *Teaching Democracy* (a collection of models for democratic citizenship and human rights education);

– *Living in Democracy* (EDC/HRE lesson plans for lower secondary level);

– *Exploring Children's Rights* (nine short projects for primary level).

The Council of Europe has also produced materials for non-formal education in the fields of EDC/HRE which have been widely translated and disseminated, for example *Compass: A Manual on Human Rights Education with Young People*.

4. Bilateral support

While most of the Council of Europe's work is multilateral, some bilateral assistance has been conducted in this field through joint programmes with the European

Union, in particular in Bosnia and Herzegovina and more recently in Kosovo.[18] Through the network of EDC/HRE co-ordinators, support on specific questions (for example curricula, teacher education) is provided by the Council of Europe to its member states on a regular basis.

5. Inter-institutional co-operation

The Council of Europe works closely with other major organisations working in the field of citizenship and human rights education in order to avoid overlap and create synergies. For instance, it was agreed with the United Nations that the Council of Europe would support in Europe the implementation of the UN World Programme for Human Rights Education, adopted by the UN General Assembly in 2005. In this framework a Regional European Meeting on the World Programme for Human Rights Education was organised by the Council of Europe and its partner institutions in 2007. The European Commission has repeatedly asked for Council of Europe assistance in this field, including recently when developing indicators for active citizenship. Other examples include the publication of *Human Rights Education in the School Systems of Europe, Central Asia and North America: A Compendium of Good Practice,* prepared jointly by the Council of Europe, the Office for Democratic Institutions and Human Rights of the Organization for Security and Co-operation in Europe (OSCE/ODIHR), the United Nations Educational, Scientific and Cultural Organization (UNESCO) and the UN Office of the High Commissioner for Human Rights (OHCHR).

The Council of Europe regularly hosts and organises inter-institutional meetings on EDC/HRE where 20 major international organisations, NGOs and foundations meet. The last meeting was organised in June 2009 and focused on teacher education.

In May 2009, the Norwegian Government inaugurated, in Oslo, the European Wergeland Centre, a European resource centre on education for intercultural under-standing, human rights and democratic citizenship which has been set up in close co-operation with the Council of Europe and which will be governed jointly by the Council of Europe and the Norwegian Government.

18. All reference to Kosovo, whether to the territory, institutions or population, in this text shall be understood in full compliance with United Nations Security Council Resolution 1244 and without prejudice to the status of Kosovo.

Appendix IV

A sample of Council of Europe materials

1. Education for democratic citizenship and human rights

The authors of *Democratic governance of schools*, both of them heads of secondary schools, describe how the journey down the road towards democracy tends to take shape, help readers to estimate how far their school has travelled so far, and offer practical advice on starting, continuing and evaluating the journey. Further materials on this topic include *Advancing democratic practice: a self-assessment guide for higher education* (2009) and *European Handbook – Promoting Democratic Schools* (2009), which was published by the Network of European Foundations in co-operation with the Council of Europe, and is aimed at out-of-school actors, such as local authorities and civil society organisations.

How all teachers can support citizenship and human rights education: a framework for the development of competences sets out the core competences needed by teachers to put democratic citizenship and human rights into practice in the classroom, school and in the wider community. It is intended for all teachers – not only specialists but teachers in all subject areas – and teacher educators working in higher education institutions or other settings, both in pre- and in-service training.

The *Tool for Quality Assurance of Education for Democratic Citizenship in Schools* was prepared as a response to the compliance gap between policies and practices of EDC in various countries. While EDC policies are well developed, EDC practices in schools present significant weaknesses. The tool was also prepared as part of the current interest and implementation of quality assurance in education. Quality assurance is a powerful means to improve the effectiveness of education. Its key principle is that the main actors at the forefront of education – such as teachers, head teachers and other stakeholders at school level (students, parents, school administrators and other staff, members of school governing bodies, the community) – are responsible for improving educational performance.

Therefore, at the centre of quality assurance are school self-evaluation and development planning processes. However, these processes are not sufficient for ensuring improvement. They need to be part of a fully fledged quality assurance system in which the national education authorities create the conditions and provide the support for performance improvement by schools. This tool is designed as a reference document. It focuses on education for democratic citizenship and applies the principles and processes of quality assurance to EDC.

The publication *Policy Tool for EDC/HRE: Strategic Support for Decision Makers* will be published in mid-2010.

Human Rights Education

in the School Systems of Europe, Central Asia and North America:

A Compendium of Good Practice

Human Rights Education in the School Systems of Europe, Central Asia and North America: A Compendium of Good Practice is a compilation of 101 examples of good practice in human rights education in primary schools, secondary schools and teacher training institutions in the Organization for Security and Co-operation in Europe (OSCE) area, which is also covered by the United Nations Educational, Scientific and Cultural Organization (UNESCO), the Office of the United Nations High Commissioner for Human Rights (OHCHR) and, partially, the geographical mandate of the Council of Europe.

The term "human rights education" is often used in this resource in a broader sense, to also include education for democratic citizenship and education for mutual respect and understanding, which are all based on internationally agreed human rights standards. These three areas are seen as interconnected and essential within educational systems in order to prepare youth to be active, responsible and caring participants in their communities, as well as at the national and global levels. Human rights education has been defined as education, training and information aimed at building a universal culture of human rights. A comprehensive education in human rights not only provides knowledge about human rights and the mechanisms that protect them, but also imparts the skills needed to promote, defend and apply human rights in daily life. Education for democratic citizenship focuses on educational practices and activities designed to help young people and adults to play an active part in democratic life and exercise their rights and responsibilities in society. Education for mutual respect and understanding highlights self-respect, respect for others, and the improvement of relationships between people of differing cultural traditions.

This book aims to support quality teaching in these areas and to inspire educational policymakers (those working in education ministries and local school boards) and administrators teachers, teacher trainers, non-formal educators and all other interested actors, as well as to facilitate networking and an exchange of experiences among education professionals.

A series of manuals for teachers on citizenship and human rights education has been published by the Council of Europe with the support of the Swiss Government and Zurich University of Teacher Education. The manuals provide step-by-step instructions and include student handouts and background information for teachers. In this way, the manual is suited for trainees or beginners in the teaching profession and teachers who are receiving in-service teacher training in education for democratic citizenship and human rights. Experienced teachers may draw on the ideas and materials.

The manuals of the series are:

Volume I: *Educating for democracy: Background materials on democratic citizenship and human rights education for teachers* (2010)

Volume II: *Growing up in democracy: Lesson plans for primary level on democratic citizenship and human rights* (2010)

Volume III: *Living in democracy: EDC/HRE Lesson plans for lower secondary level* (2008)

Volume IV: *Taking part in democracy: Lesson plans for upper secondary level on democratic citizenship and human rights* (2010)

Volume V: *Exploring children's rights: nine short projects for primary level* (2007)

Volume VI: *Teaching democracy: a collection of models for democratic citizenship and human rights education* (2009)

Further information and downloadable versions are available at www.coe.int/edc.

A teaching pack for secondary schools entitled *The European Convention on Human Rights – starting points for teachers* aims to introduce human rights into the classroom by providing starting points and suggesting some interactive activities. The pack is designed primarily for working with students. Constructed in the form of a folder, the teaching pack contains five basic information sheets on the Convention and the human rights work of the Council of Europe and ten sheets with suggestions for classroom activities on human rights education. The classroom activities sheets place an emphasis on relating human rights standards to school students' everyday lives. The pack is also available on a CD-Rom containing 24 language editions.

Online versions (text only) are available at www.coe.int/edc. Copies of the folders in French, English, German, Russian, Italian and Spanish can be obtained free of charge from: infopoint@coe.int.

The Council of Europe has published a new teaching pack for secondary schools – to replace the original – to celebrate the 60th anniversary of the European Convention on Human Rights in 2010. It is entitled "Europe is more than you think".

2. Religious diversity and intercultural education

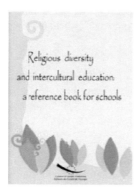

The religious dimension of intercultural education is an issue that affects all schools, whether they are religiously diverse or not, because their pupils live and will work in increasingly diverse societies. *Religious diversity and intercultural education: a reference book for schools* is intended primarily for teachers, teacher administrators and policy makers and includes theoretical perspectives and examples of current practice. The publication can be ordered at www.coe.int/edc.

3. History teaching

Multiperspectivity, described by Dr Robert Stradling in *Multiperspectivity in History Teachings: a Guide for Teachers* published by the Council of Europe in 2003, is a method for teaching history that has proved its efficiency in present-day schools. This method permits historical events to be viewed from several perspectives. It can also extend the scope of the historical account by examining how the different perspectives relate to each other. The Council of Europe's experience shows that this method can help teachers develop interactive teaching processes and their pupils to acquire skills such as keeping an open mind, thinking critically and analysing facts by coming to independent conclusions that are crucial in becoming responsible and active citizens. The guide is available in 17 languages. The publication can be downloaded at www.book.coe.int.

The Black Sea: A History of Interactions is a teaching pack that provides information for schools that will help teachers and pupils to learn more about the history of the countries belonging to this geographical area, as well as about the Black Sea region itself. It is the first time specialists from Bulgaria, Georgia, the Republic of Moldova, Romania, the Russian Federation, Turkey and Ukraine, under the auspices of the Council of Europe, have created a historical picture of the Black Sea. The Council of Europe has always supported the view that diversity and intercultural dialogue are enriching factors in the building of mutual understanding in the present-day world. One of the main ideas when preparing the teaching pack was to show new approaches to teaching history in its full complexity on the basis of multiperspectivity and compara-tive study. The teaching pack is available in English. Further information is available at www.coe.int/historyteaching.

The publication *Crossroads of European histories – Multiple outlooks on five key moments in the history of Europe* (2007), accompanied by a CD-Rom and a pedagogical handbook, is a contribution to the implementation of a methodology based on multiperspectivity and allows teachers to present numerous examples of different approaches in their practical teaching, as well as different points of view on the same events in recent European history. Thirty-five of the contributions published in this book are from eminent historians from different member states within the framework of Council of Europe confer-ences. This publication allows teachers and pupils to place regional and national history in a wider context, to develop their historical knowledge, to make connections across space and time, and to compare different perspectives on the same events and developments.

The publication is available in English and in French and can be ordered at www.book.coe.int.

4. Roma education

The *Factsheet on Roma History* is addressed to teachers, pupils, decision makers and experts, and can be used in all teaching contexts. This publication was produced with the financial support of the Finnish Ministry of Foreign Affairs. *Access to education: teaching kit concept* (2007) outlines guidelines for preparing Roma, Sinti and Traveller children who have not attended nursery school for entry into the first year of primary school. Further information, including the factsheet in English, French and Romani, can be found at www.coe.int/education/roma.

5. Youth

Compass is a manual on human rights education for youth, and *Compasito* is a manual on human rights education for children aged 7-13. These books are addressed to educators, teachers and trainers. Primarily developed for non-formal education settings, they can also be used in formal education. They familiarise the reader with the key concepts of human rights and children's rights, provide substantial theoretical background to key human rights issues and propose numerous activities. The manuals can be ordered at www.coe.int/edc.

Compass, Compasito and other related materials (such as the manual *Gender Matters* and the *All Equal – All Different* education pack) can be downloaded in multiple languages at http://eycb.coe.int/compass/.

Appendix V

Author biographies

Matt Hartley

Matt Hartley is Associate Professor of Education at the University of Pennsylvania's Graduate School of Education where he serves as the Chair of the Higher Education Division. His research and writing examine how colleges and universities define their educational missions and he has been particularly interested in examining the civic purposes of colleges and universities – their roles in their communities and their contributions to a strong democracy. Matt has been a reviewer for many scholarly journals and academic presses and serves on the editorial boards of the *Review of Higher Education* and the *Journal of Higher Education Outreach and Engagement*.

Ted Huddleston

Ted Huddleston has worked in education in a number of different capacities – as a classroom teacher, teacher educator, researcher and writer. His main area of interest is citizenship and human rights education, nationally and internationally – including policy and curriculum development, teacher training and resource creation. He has worked in a number of countries, such as Bosnia and Herzegovina, Serbia, Kosovo, Bahrain, Turkey, Oman and Ethiopia. He is the author and co-author of a number of education books and teaching resources, for example: *Good Thinking: Education for Citizenship and Moral Responsibility* (2001); *Changing Places: Young People and Community Action* (2002); *Citizens and Society: A Political Literacy Resource Pack* (2004); *Making Sense of Citizenship: A Continuing Professional Development Handbook* (2006); *Identity Diversity and Citizenship: A Critical Review of Educational Resources* (2007); *Placing Citizenship at the Centre: Developing a Citizenship Manifesto for your School* (2008); *Citizenship and Religious Education* (2009) and *Schools for Society: Learning Democracy in Europe – A Handbook of Ideas for Action* (2009). After many years with the Citizenship Foundation in London, Ted now works as a freelance educational consultant and is a contributor to the Council of Europe's Education for Democratic Citizenship and Human Rights Education programme.

Sales agents for publications of the Council of Europe
Agents de vente des publications du Conseil de l'Europe

BELGIUM/BELGIQUE
La Librairie Européenne -
The European Bookshop
Rue de l'Orme, 1
BE-1040 BRUXELLES
Tel.: +32 (0)2 231 04 35
Fax: +32 (0)2 735 08 60
E-mail: order@libeurop.be
http://www.libeurop.be

Jean De Lannoy/DL Services
Avenue du Roi 202 Koningslaan
BE-1190 BRUXELLES
Tel.: +32 (0)2 538 43 08
Fax: +32 (0)2 538 08 41
E-mail: jean.de.lannoy@dl-servi.com
http://www.jean-de-lannoy.be

**BOSNIA AND HERZEGOVINA/
BOSNIE-HERZÉGOVINE**
Robert's Plus d.o.o.
Marka Maruliça 2/V
BA-71000, SARAJEVO
Tel.: + 387 33 640 818
Fax: + 387 33 640 818
E-mail: robertsplus@bih.net.ba

CANADA
Renouf Publishing Co. Ltd.
1-5369 Canotek Road
CA-OTTAWA, Ontario K1J 9J3
Tel.: +1 613 745 2665
Fax: +1 613 745 7660
Toll-Free Tel.: (866) 767-6766
E-mail: order.dept@renoufbooks.com
http://www.renoufbooks.com

CROATIA/CROATIE
Robert's Plus d.o.o.
Marasoviçeva 67
HR-21000, SPLIT
Tel.: + 385 21 315 800, 801, 802, 803
Fax: + 385 21 315 804
E-mail: robertsplus@robertsplus.hr

**CZECH REPUBLIC/
RÉPUBLIQUE TCHÈQUE**
Suweco CZ, s.r.o.
Klecakova 347
CZ-180 21 PRAHA 9
Tel.: +420 2 424 59 204
Fax: +420 2 848 21 646
E-mail: import@suweco.cz
http://www.suweco.cz

DENMARK/DANEMARK
GAD
Vimmelskaftet 32
DK-1161 KØBENHAVN K
Tel.: +45 77 66 60 00
Fax: +45 77 66 60 01
E-mail: gad@gad.dk
http://www.gad.dk

FINLAND/FINLANDE
Akateeminen Kirjakauppa
PO Box 128
Keskuskatu 1
FI-00100 HELSINKI
Tel.: +358 (0)9 121 4430
Fax: +358 (0)9 121 4242
E-mail: akatilaus@akateeminen.com
http://www.akateeminen.com

FRANCE
La Documentation française
(diffusion/distribution France entière)
124, rue Henri Barbusse
FR-93308 AUBERVILLIERS CEDEX
Tél.: +33 (0)1 40 15 70 00
Fax: +33 (0)1 40 15 68 00
E-mail: commande@ladocumentationfrancaise.fr
http://www.ladocumentationfrancaise.fr

Librairie Kléber
1 rue des Francs Bourgeois
FR-67000 STRASBOURG
Tel.: +33 (0)3 88 15 78 88
Fax: +33 (0)3 88 15 78 80
E-mail: librairie-kleber@coe.int
http://www.librairie-kleber.com

**GERMANY/ALLEMAGNE
AUSTRIA/AUTRICHE**
UNO Verlag GmbH
August-Bebel-Allee 6
DE-53175 BONN
Tel.: +49 (0)228 94 90 20
Fax: +49 (0)228 94 90 222
E-mail: bestellung@uno-verlag.de
http://www.uno-verlag.de

GREECE/GRÈCE
Librairie Kauffmann s.a.
Stadiou 28
GR-105 64 ATHINAI
Tel.: +30 210 32 55 321
Fax.: +30 210 32 30 320
E-mail: ord@otenet.gr
http://www.kauffmann.gr

HUNGARY/HONGRIE
Euro Info Service
Pannónia u. 58.
PF. 1039
HU-1136 BUDAPEST
Tel.: +36 1 329 2170
Fax: +36 1 349 2053
E-mail: euroinfo@euroinfo.hu
http://www.euroinfo.hu

ITALY/ITALIE
Licosa SpA
Via Duca di Calabria, 1/1
IT-50125 FIRENZE
Tel.: +39 0556 483215
Fax: +39 0556 41257
E-mail: licosa@licosa.com
http://www.licosa.com

MEXICO/MEXIQUE
Mundi-Prensa México, S.A. De C.V.
Río Pánuco, 141 Delegacíon Cuauhtémoc
MX-06500 MÉXICO, D.F.
Tel.: +52 (01)55 55 33 56 58
Fax: +52 (01)55 55 14 67 99
E-mail: mundiprensa@mundiprensa.com.mx
http://www.mundiprensa.com.mx

NETHERLANDS/PAYS-BAS
Roodveldt Import BV
Nieuwe Hemweg 50
NE-1013 CX AMSTERDAM
Tel.: + 31 20 622 8035
Fax.: + 31 20 625 5493
Website: www.publidis.org
Email: orders@publidis.org

NORWAY/NORVÈGE
Akademika
Postboks 84 Blindern
NO-0314 OSLO
Tel.: +47 2 218 8100
Fax: +47 2 218 8103
E-mail: support@akademika.no
http://www.akademika.no

POLAND/POLOGNE
Ars Polona JSC
25 Obroncow Street
PL-03-933 WARSZAWA
Tel.: +48 (0)22 509 86 00
Fax: +48 (0)22 509 86 10
E-mail: arspolona@arspolona.com.pl
http://www.arspolona.com.pl

PORTUGAL
Livraria Portugal
(Dias & Andrade, Lda.)
Rua do Carmo, 70
PT-1200-094 LISBOA
Tel.: +351 21 347 42 82 / 85
Fax: +351 21 347 02 64
E-mail: info@livrariaportugal.pt
http://www.livrariaportugal.pt

**RUSSIAN FEDERATION/
FÉDÉRATION DE RUSSIE**
Ves Mir
17b, Butlerova ul.
RU-101000 MOSCOW
Tel.: +7 495 739 0971
Fax: +7 495 739 0971
E-mail: orders@vesmirbooks.ru
http://www.vesmirbooks.ru

SPAIN/ESPAGNE
Mundi-Prensa Libros, s.a.
Castelló, 37
ES-28001 MADRID
Tel.: +34 914 36 37 00
Fax: +34 915 75 39 98
E-mail: libreria@mundiprensa.es
http://www.mundiprensa.com

SWITZERLAND/SUISSE
Planetis Sàrl
16 chemin des Pins
CH-1273 ARZIER
Tel.: +41 22 366 51 77
Fax: +41 22 366 51 78
E-mail: info@planetis.ch

UNITED KINGDOM/ROYAUME-UNI
The Stationery Office Ltd
PO Box 29
GB-NORWICH NR3 1GN
Tel.: +44 (0)870 600 5522
Fax: +44 (0)870 600 5533
E-mail: book.enquiries@tso.co.uk
http://www.tsoshop.co.uk

**UNITED STATES and CANADA/
ÉTATS-UNIS et CANADA**
Manhattan Publishing Co
2036 Albany Post Road
USA-10520 CROTON ON HUDSON, NY
Tel.: +1 914 271 5194
Fax: +1 914 271 5886
E-mail: coe@manhattanpublishing.coe
http://www.manhattanpublishing.com

Council of Europe Publishing/Editions du Conseil de l'Europe
FR-67075 STRASBOURG Cedex
Tel.: +33 (0)3 88 41 25 81 – Fax: +33 (0)3 88 41 39 10 – E-mail: publishing@coe.int – Website: http://book.coe.int